CHARTOGRAPHY

THE WEIRD AND WONDERFUL
WORLD OF INFOGRAPHICS

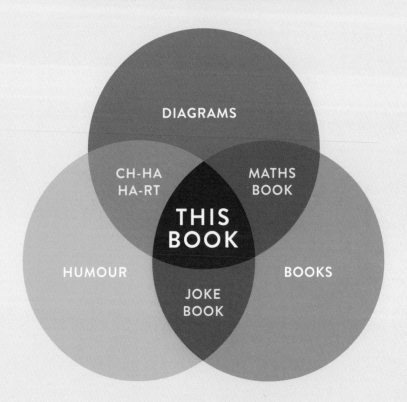

DIAGRAMS

CH-HA HA-RT

MATHS BOOK

THIS BOOK

HUMOUR

BOOKS

JOKE BOOK

STEPHEN WILDISH

summersdale

CHARTOGRAPHY

Summersdale Publishers Ltd
46 West Street
Chichester
West Sussex
PO19 1RP
UK

www.summersdale.com

Printed and bound in China

ISBN: 978-1-84953-919-7

Substantial discounts on bulk quantities of Summersdale books are available to corporations, professional associations and other organisations. For details contact Nicky Douglas by telephone: +44 (0) 1243 756902, fax: +44 (0) 1243 786300 or email: nicky@summersdale.com.

INTRODUCTION

Chartography is essentially a collection
of nonsense mixed with a tiny amount
of real facts. I'm afraid you will have to
work out for yourself which is which.

PEC

OPLE

HOLY VENN DIAGRAM, BATMAN

A Venn diagram exploring the relationship between bats and humankind. Which only leaves the question, 'When will Wombat Man become real?'

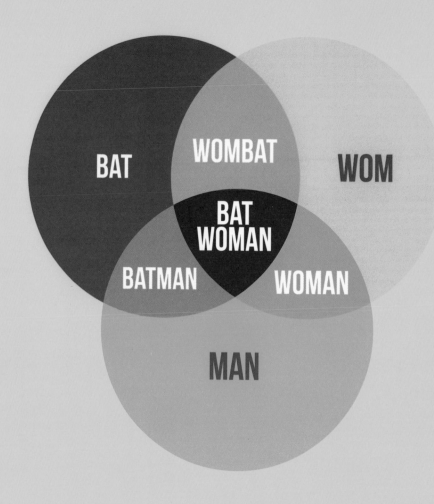

DER MAN SPI

With great power comes great responsibility, and also a fancy leotard.

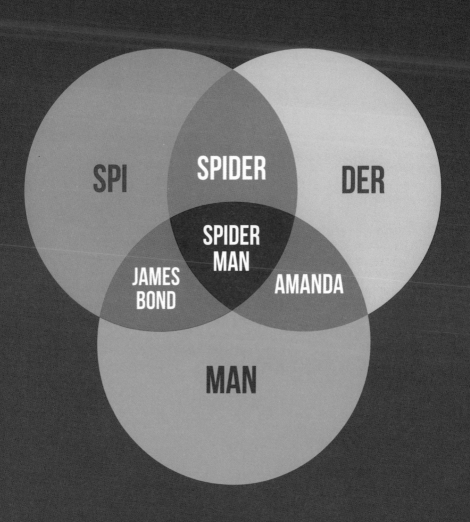

SPI

SPIDER

DER

SPIDER MAN

JAMES BOND

AMANDA

MAN

THE HUMAN SENSES

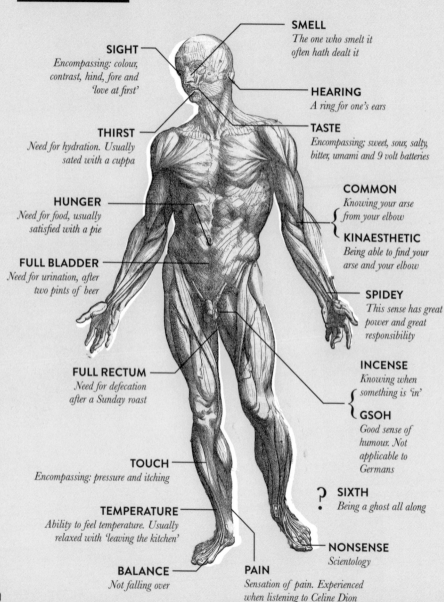

SMELL
The one who smelt it often hath dealt it

SIGHT
Encompassing: colour, contrast, hind, fore and 'love at first'

HEARING
A ring for one's ears

THIRST
Need for hydration. Usually sated with a cuppa

TASTE
Encompassing; sweet, sour, salty, bitter, umami and 9 volt batteries

COMMON
Knowing your arse from your elbow

HUNGER
Need for food, usually satisfied with a pie

KINAESTHETIC
Being able to find your arse and your elbow

FULL BLADDER
Need for urination, after two pints of beer

SPIDEY
This sense has great power and great responsibility

INCENSE
Knowing when something is 'in'

FULL RECTUM
Need for defecation after a Sunday roast

GSOH
Good sense of humour. Not applicable to Germans

TOUCH
Encompassing: pressure and itching

? SIXTH
Being a ghost all along

TEMPERATURE
Ability to feel temperature. Usually relaxed with 'leaving the kitchen'

NONSENSE
Scientology

BALANCE
Not falling over

PAIN
Sensation of pain. Experienced when listening to Celine Dion

MAGICAL WHITE BEARDS

The longer the beard, the more magical.

MAGICAL POWERS

BEARD LENGTH

MARX

SANTA

DUMBLEDORE

SARUMAN

GANDALF

WELL, WELL, WELLES

GEORGE ORWELL	H.G. WELLS	ORSON WELLES

Spanish Civil **WAR**	Wrote	Performed

WAR OF THE WORLDS

Citizen Smith	*The Ideal Citizen*	*Citizen Kane*

SOCIALIST IDEALS

Dystopian	Utopian	Rosebud

SCIENCE FICTION   **?**

Wrote	Divorced	Died
1984	**1894**	**198...5**

TOMS RANKED BY HEIGHT

At 1.83 m, Tom Hanks towers over the diminutive Tom Cruise.

BIG

NOT UNUSUAL

COCKTAIL

BOUFFANTS OF POWER

In the twentieth century and beyond, the biggest bouffants that have held maximum power per decade.

LIZ

TINA

MAGGIE

1960s   1970s   1980s

OPRAH

HILLARY

ANGELA

1990s   2000s   2010s

CH-CH-CHANGES

The king of changes through the decades.

THE CHANGING HAIR OF BRAD PITT

The correlation between Brad's hair length and sex appeal.

SEX APPEAL

THELMA
& LOUISE

SEVEN

SNATCH

WORLD
WAR Z

LEGENDS
OF THE FALL

HAIR LENGTH

A CHILD'S AVERAGE DAY

A child's day hasn't changed much since 1816...

INDUSTRIAL REVOLUTION

MINING

DIGITAL REVOLUTION

MINECRAFT

BONDS RANKED BY EYEBROW DEXTERITY

One Bond rules the roost when it comes to eyebrow dexterity...

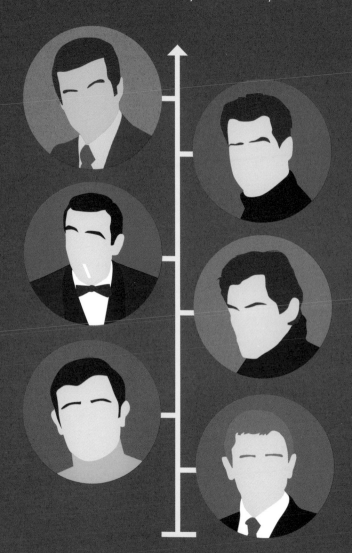

BOBS RANKED BY HAIR NEATNESS

From neat to scruffy, three Bobs ranked by the neatness of their 'fros.

ROSS
HAPPY, LITTLE CLOUD

DYLAN
BLOWIN' IN THE WIND

GELDOF
BOOMTOWN RAT

A TALE OF TWO CHARLIES

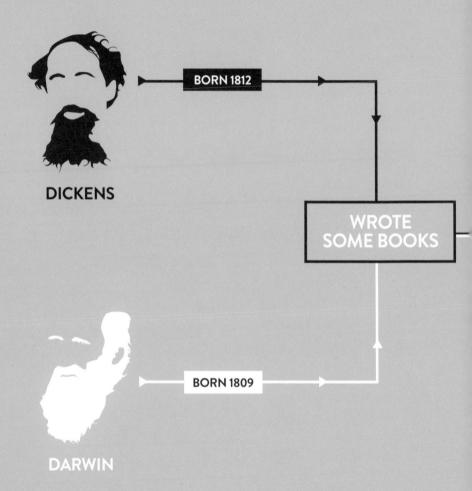

DICKENS

BORN 1812

WROTE
SOME BOOKS

BORN 1809

DARWIN

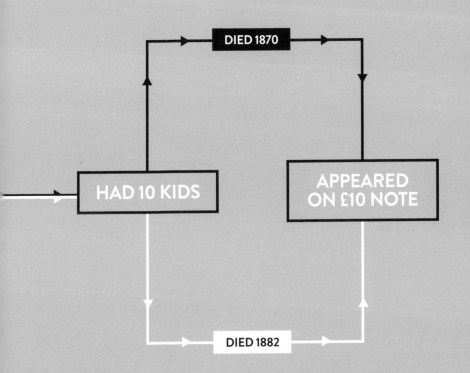

DIED 1870

HAD 10 KIDS

APPEARED ON £10 NOTE

DIED 1882

MONET, MANET, MANRAY

The lives of Monet, Manet and Man Ray and had some interesting junctions.

WOULD BE FUNNAY...

MONET

MANET

MAN RAY

The birth of
IMPRESSIONISM

Did some
PAINTINGS

Took some
PHOTOS

TWO WIVES

Married
1863

DIED AGED 86

THE VON VAN VENN

Very!

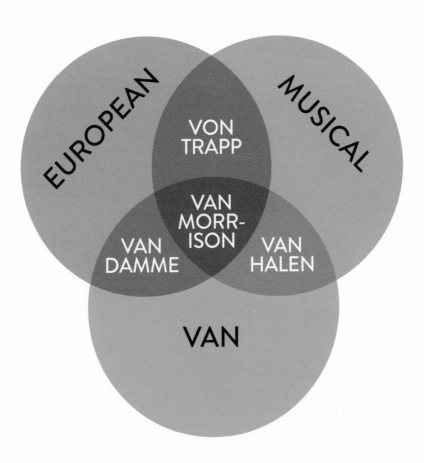

EUROPEAN

MUSICAL

VON TRAPP

VAN MORR-ISON

VAN DAMME

VAN HALEN

VAN

THE SAXON FIVE

Don't blame it on the moonlight, blame it on the North Sea.
Fresh from their eighth-century tour of Britain.

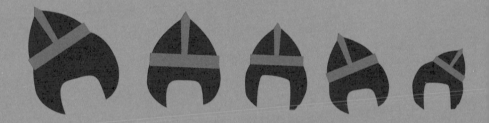

BARRYS

From falsetto to bass, the kings of 'back to mine for coffee' music ranked by the pitch of their voice.

MORE THAN A WOMAN

MANDY

THE WALRUS OF LOVE

MULLET

Business up front and party at the back.

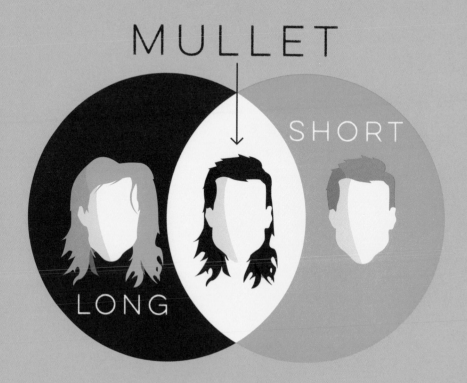

GOATEE

When a soul patch and a handlebar moustache are
very much in love they have a special cuddle, known as a goatee.

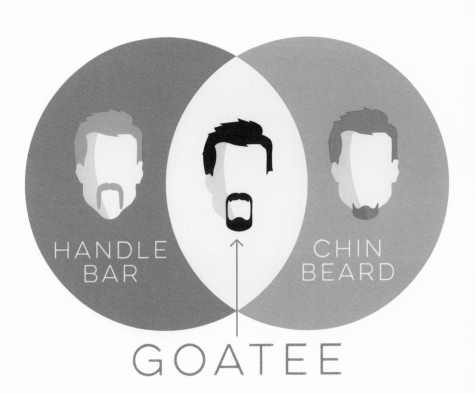

HANDLE
BAR

CHIN
BEARD

GOATEE

MOONWALK VENN

Cab Calloway accidentally performed the moonwalk in 1932 after attempting to wipe dog's mess from the sole of his shoes.

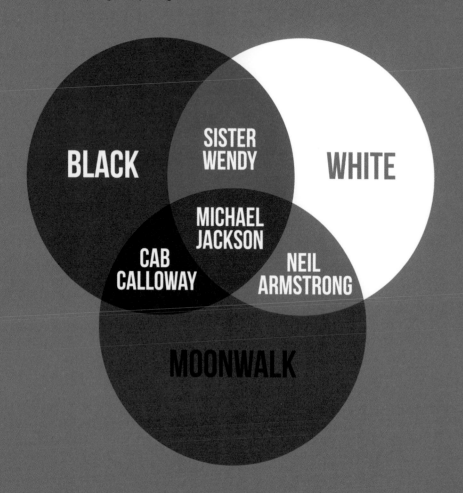

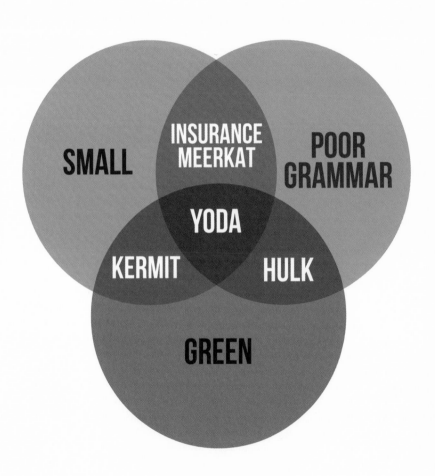

FO

WHAT TO HAVE FOR TEA?

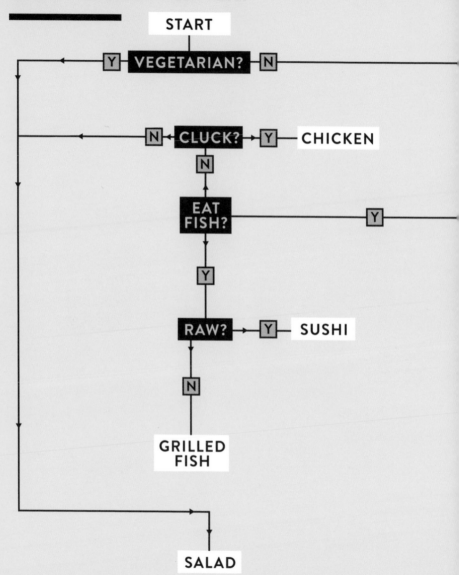

START

VEGETARIAN?

Y

N

CLUCK?

N

Y

CHICKEN

N

EAT FISH?

Y

Y

RAW?

Y

SUSHI

N

GRILLED FISH

SALAD

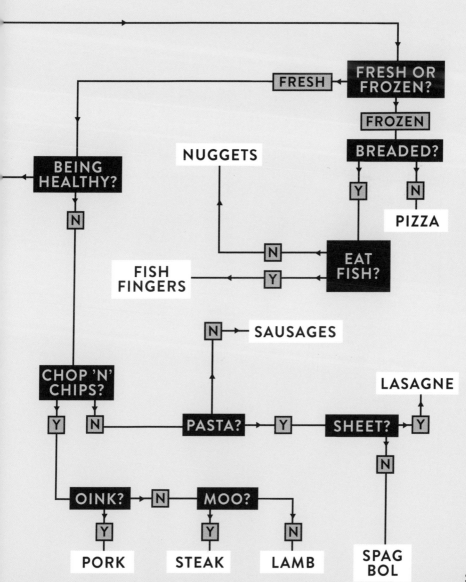

FRESH OR FROZEN?

FRESH

FROZEN

BREADED?

Y

N

PIZZA

NUGGETS

BEING HEALTHY?

N

EAT FISH?

N

Y

FISH FINGERS

SAUSAGES

N

LASAGNE

CHOP 'N' CHIPS?

Y

N

PASTA?

Y

SHEET?

Y

N

OINK?

N

MOO?

Y

N

N

PORK

STEAK

LAMB

SPAG BOL

35

THE IMPORTANCE OF COLOUR

Before you tuck into that tasty croissant,
just double check that it is not, in fact, a human beard.

 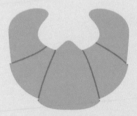

BEARD   CROISSANT

BACON CAKE

What's better than cake? Bacon. What's better than Bacon? Bacon cake.

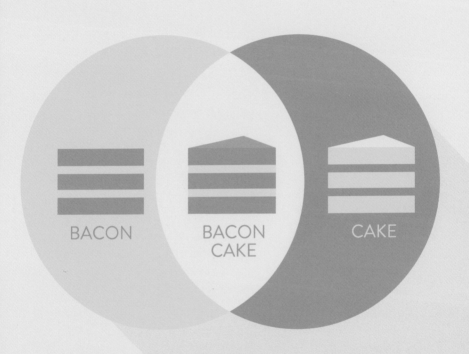

BACON

BACON
CAKE

CAKE

BRITISH COCKTAILS

LEMONADE

LAGER

LAGER TOP

LIME

LAGER

LAGER & LIME

BLACKCURRANT

GUINNESS

GUINNESS & BLACK

LAGER

LEMONADE

LAGER SHANDY

BITTER

LEMONADE

BITTER SHANDY

BLACKCURRANT

CIDER

CIDER & BLACK

LAGER

CIDER

SNAKEBITE

BLACKCURRANT

CIDER

LAGER

DIESEL

BLACKCURRANT
VODKA

CIDER

LAGER

TURBO DIESEL

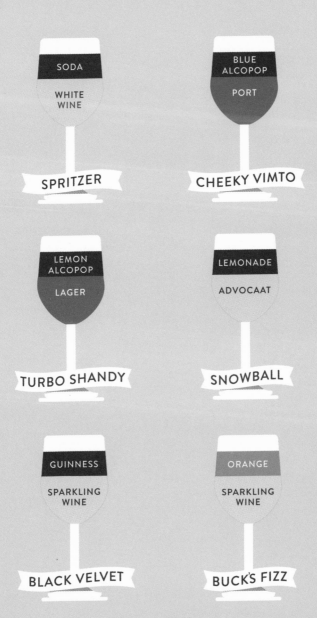

SODA

WHITE WINE

SPRITZER

BLUE ALCOPOP

PORT

CHEEKY VIMTO

LEMON ALCOPOP

LAGER

TURBO SHANDY

LEMONADE

ADVOCAAT

SNOWBALL

GUINNESS

SPARKLING WINE

BLACK VELVET

ORANGE

SPARKLING WINE

BUCK'S FIZZ

HANGOVER COCKTAILS

Also available is a Paracetamolotov cocktail.

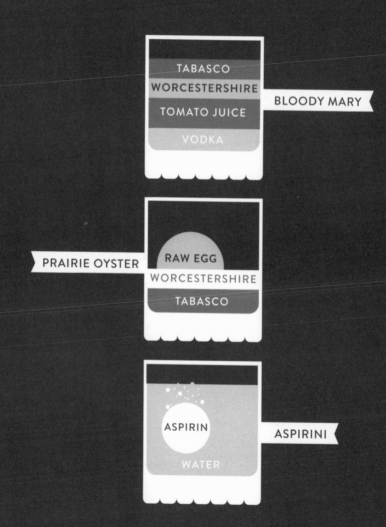

TABASCO
WORCESTERSHIRE
TOMATO JUICE
VODKA

BLOODY MARY

PRAIRIE OYSTER
RAW EGG
WORCESTERSHIRE
TABASCO

ASPIRIN
WATER

ASPIRINI

ANATOMY OF A SPROUT

Frrrrrp.

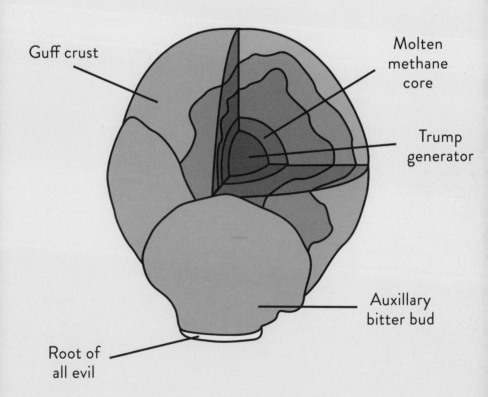

Guff crust

Molten
methane
core

Trump
generator

Auxillary
bitter bud

Root of
all evil

INNUENDOUGH

Rude bread and biscuits.

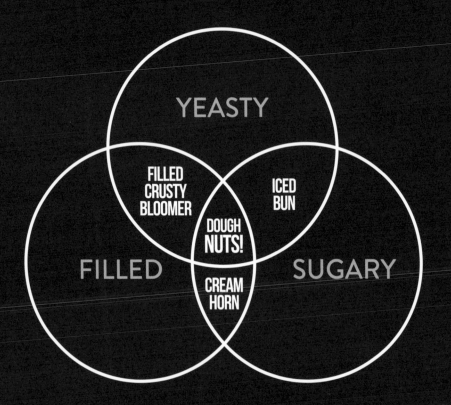

YEASTY

FILLED
CRUSTY
BLOOMER

ICED
BUN

DOUGH
NUTS!

FILLED

CREAM
HORN

SUGARY

IT TASTES LIKE CHICKEN

The legendary foods that taste like chicken.
Now to go and marinate my termite wings.

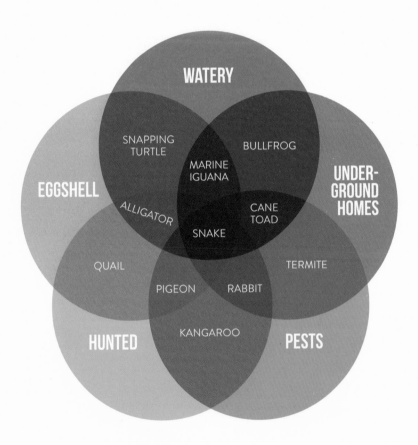

HOT-SAUCE DILEMMA

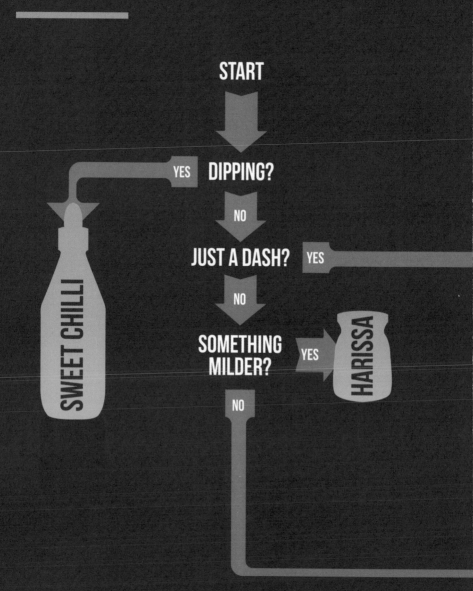

START

DIPPING? YES

NO

JUST A DASH? YES

NO

SOMETHING MILDER? YES

NO

SWEET CHILLI

HARISSA

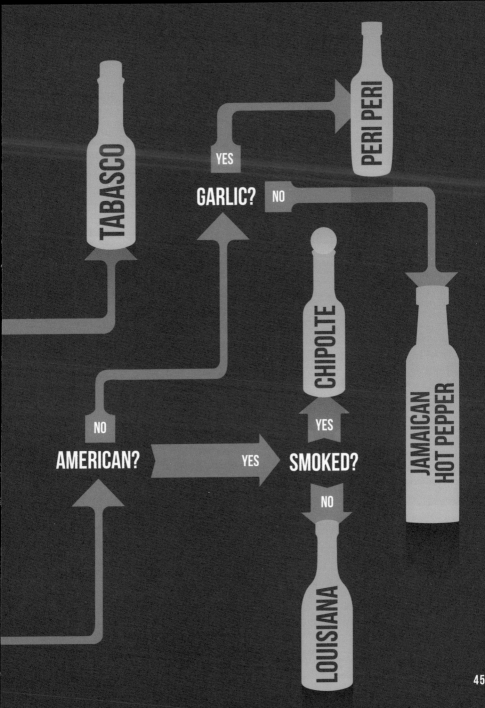

TABASCO

PERI PERI

GARLIC?

YES

NO

CHIPOLTE

JAMAICAN HOT PEPPER

NO

AMERICAN?

YES

SMOKED?

YES

NO

LOUISIANA

45

HAM THICKNESS BY POSHNESS

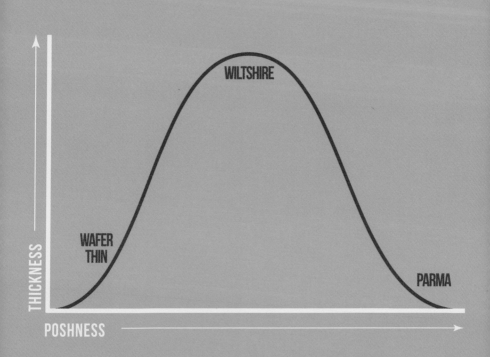

FUNGI ID CHART

Never struggle to identify edible
mushrooms again.

Porcini

Chestnut Mushroom

Chocolate Teacake

EDIBLE

Fly Agaric

Gameshow
Buzzer

Ladybird

NON-EDIBLE

SEAFOOD BY POSHNESS

Prawn ring, sir?

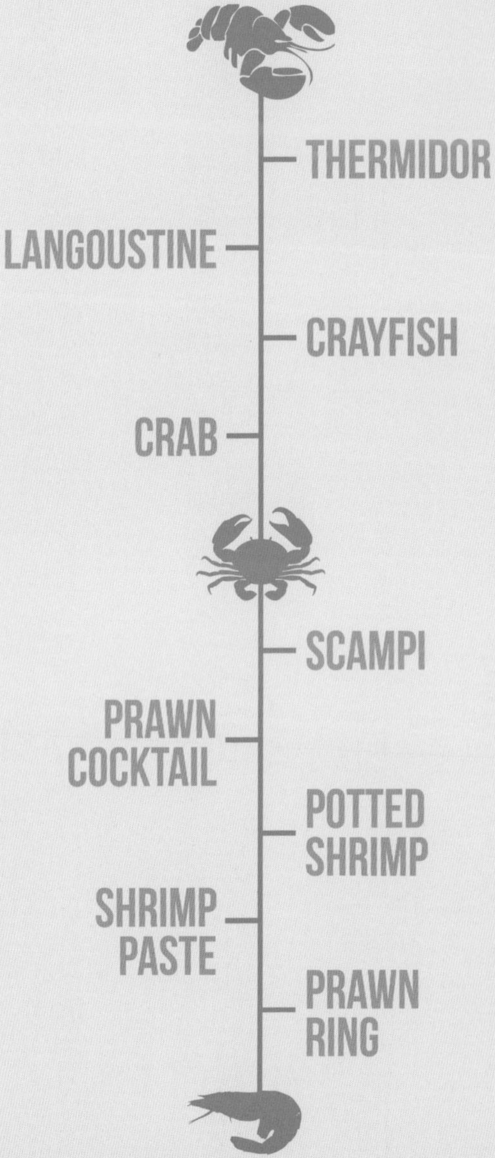

THERMIDOR

LANGOUSTINE

CRAYFISH

CRAB

SCAMPI

PRAWN
COCKTAIL

POTTED
SHRIMP

SHRIMP
PASTE

PRAWN
RING

CREAM TEA ORDERING

Jam first vs cream first.

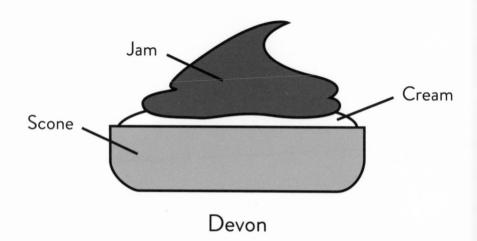

Jam

Cream

Scone

Devon

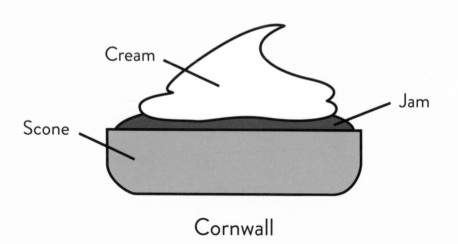

Cream

Jam

Scone

Cornwall

PASTY CRIMPS

Side crimp vs top crimp.

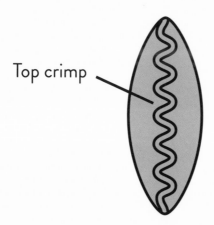

Top crimp

Devon

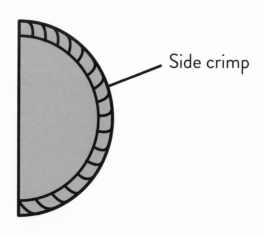

Side crimp

Cornwall

MUSTARD OR CUSTARD

Is it mustard or is it custard? A question as old as time itself.

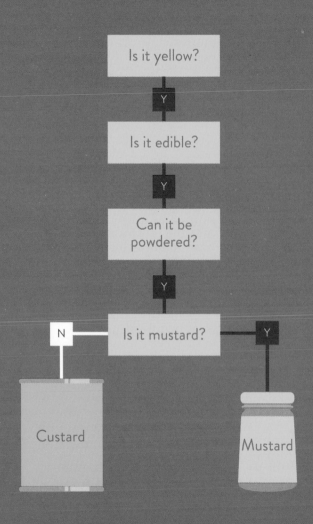

Is it yellow?

Y

Is it edible?

Y

Can it be powdered?

Y

N   Is it mustard?   Y

Custard

Mustard

MOUSTARDS

Moustards ranked by strength.

NACHO NACHO MAN

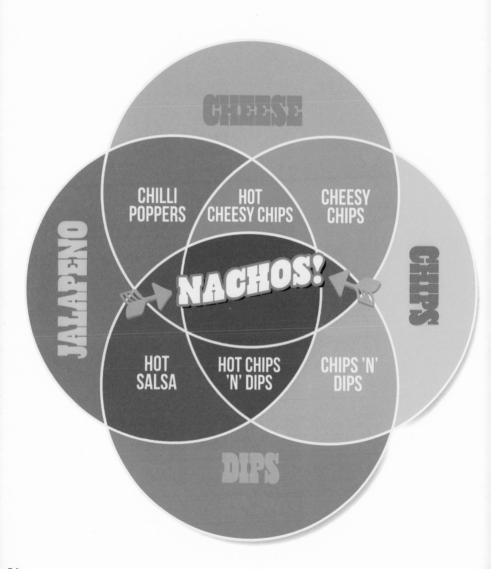

CHEESE

JALAPENO

CHIPS

DIPS

CHILLI POPPERS

HOT CHEESY CHIPS

CHEESY CHIPS

NACHOS!

HOT SALSA

HOT CHIPS 'N' DIPS

CHIPS 'N' DIPS

THE IMPORTANCE OF COLOUR

Always check...

SHERBET

DYNAMITE

SANDWICH FILLINGS BY POSHNESS

Fancy a knuckle sandwich!?

SMOKED SALMON	CUCUMBER
CRESS	**GENTLEMAN'S RELISH**
HORSERADISH	HUMMUS
BEEF	**CREAM CHEESE**
PRAWN	HONEY

MAYONNAISE	LETTUCE
TOMATO	**MARMITE**
TUNA	CHICKEN
PEANUT BUTTER	**JAM**
HAM	BACON
SWEETCORN	**PICKLE**
CHIPS	KNUCKLE
EGG	**CHEESE**
DRIPPING	SALAD CREAM

FAD FOOD FIG

It won't be long before a moustached hipster is serving you a pulled pork bap marinated in craft beer with a salt caramel and popping candy sauce from his pop-up tuk-tuk kitchen in Shoreditch.

THE ULTIMATE SANDWICH

Anatomy of the king of the sandwiches.
The triple-decker club sandwich.

BLT

CHICKEN MAYO

FIZZ THROUGH LIFE

Fizzy things follow you through life.
Current status: mid-Champagne
to vitamins.

POP

CHAMPAGNE

VITAMINS

TIME

FRENCH PICNIC

The holy trinity of fermented foods.

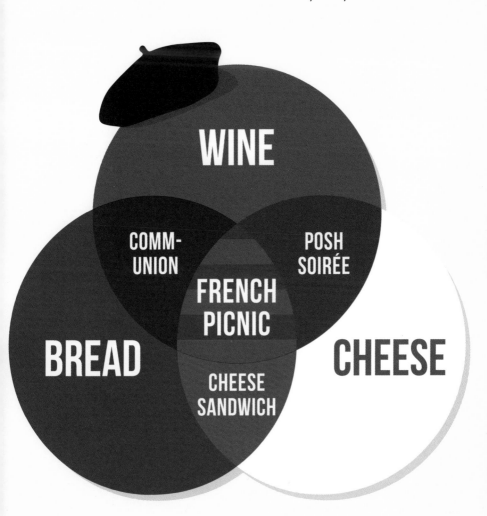

WINE

COMM-UNION

POSH SOIRÉE

FRENCH PICNIC

BREAD

CHEESE SANDWICH

CHEESE

KETCHUP MUSTARD

We can only dream of a world in which ketchup bottles have a stripe of mustard in them, much like toothpaste tubes.

MUSTARD

KETCHUP

HOT DOGAGRAM

How much of a hot dog is sausage and how much is bun?
Never wonder again.

SAUSAGE

BUN

FOOD WITH HOLES

Density by diameter.

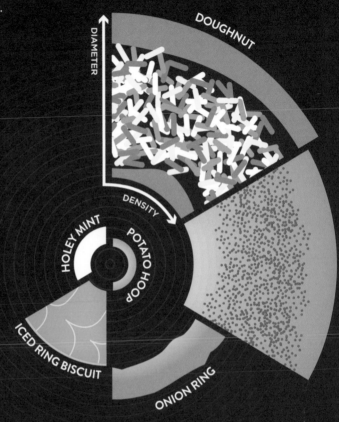

DIAMETER

DENSITY

DOUGHNUT

BAGEL

HOLEY MINT

POTATO HOOP

ICED RING BISCUIT

ONION RING

ANATOMY OF THE POTATO

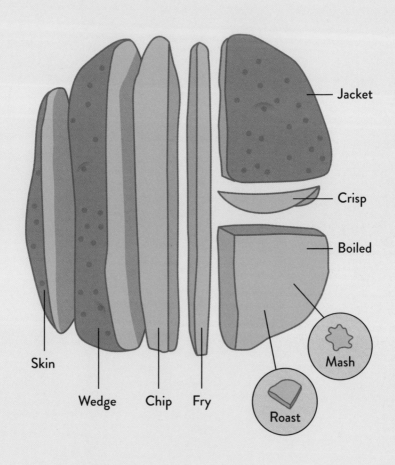

Jacket

Crisp

Boiled

Skin

Wedge

Chip

Fry

Roast

Mash

HOW TO MAKE TEA

Builder's

Posh

Hippy

TEABAG

LOOSE LEAF

LEAVES & TWIGS

ADD BOILING WATER   ADD BOILING WATER

LEAVE TO BREW   LEAVE TO BREW

ADD MILK TO CUP

4 SUGARS   POUR OUT   POUR AWAY

ORANGES ARE NOT THE ONLY FRUIT

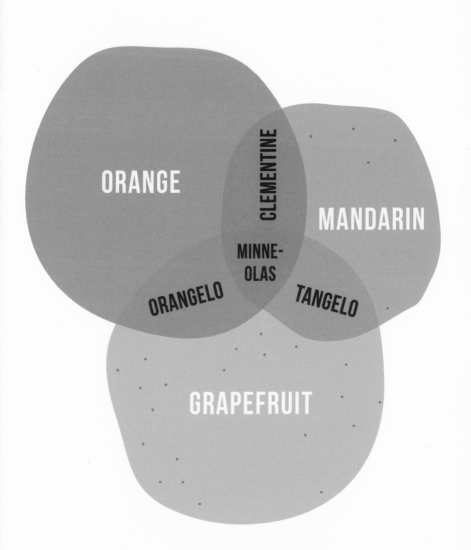

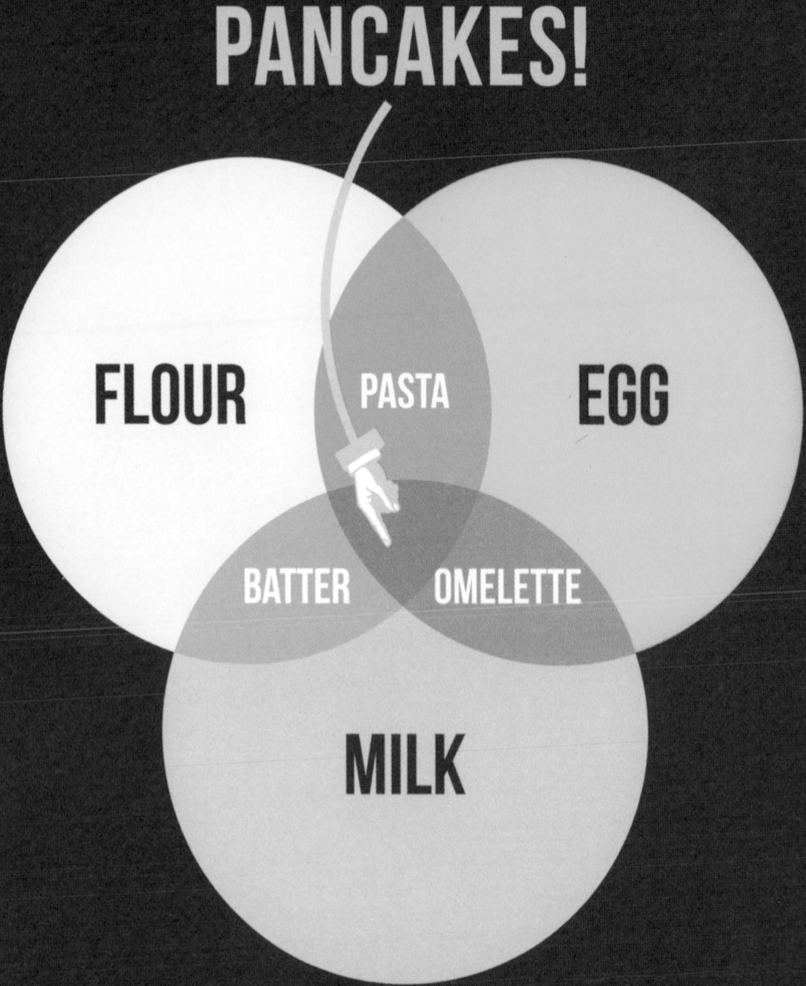

PANCAKES!

FLOUR

EGG

PASTA

BATTER OMELETTE

MILK

PIE, TART, LATTICE

American Lattice just doesn't have the same ring to it.

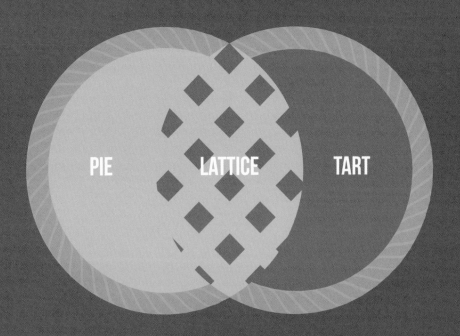

PIE   LATTICE   TART

PIZZA

Base thickness and cheese coverage over time.

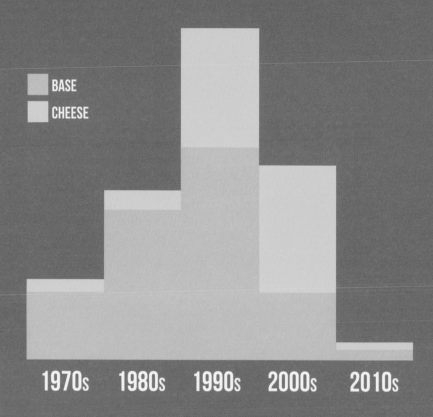

BASE

CHEESE

1970s   1980s   1990s   2000s   2010s

TOPPINGS

The inexplicable rise of rocket and demise of pineapple as a suitable pizza topping.

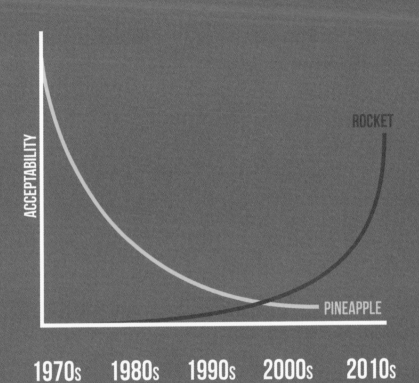

ACCEPTABILITY

ROCKET

PINEAPPLE

1970s 1980s 1990s 2000s 2010s

TEA OR COFFEE

Let this chart take the strain on this tricky decision.

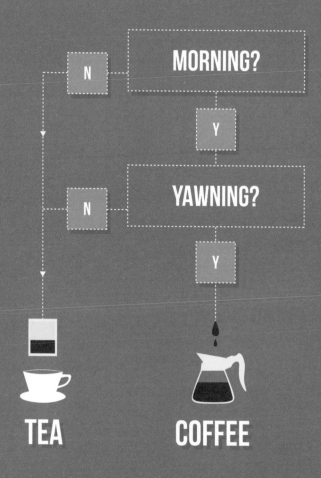

HOW TO MAKE BREAD

A simple chart for the wannabe bakers among us.

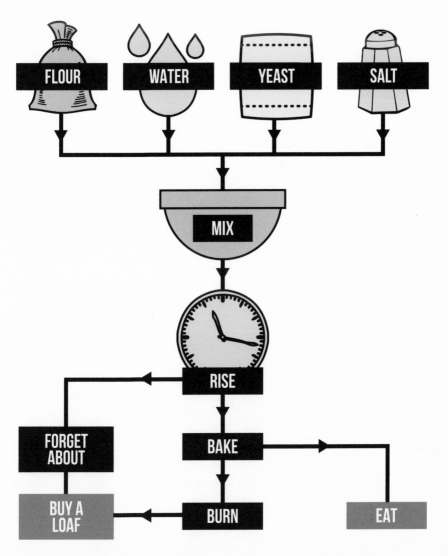

PRESERVES

Looking to make preserves but lost the recipe?
Let this chart help you out of your pickle... or jam.

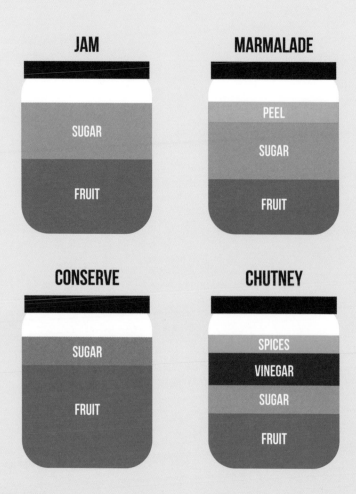

JAM
- SUGAR
- FRUIT

MARMALADE
- PEEL
- SUGAR
- FRUIT

CONSERVE
- SUGAR
- FRUIT

CHUTNEY
- SPICES
- VINEGAR
- SUGAR
- FRUIT

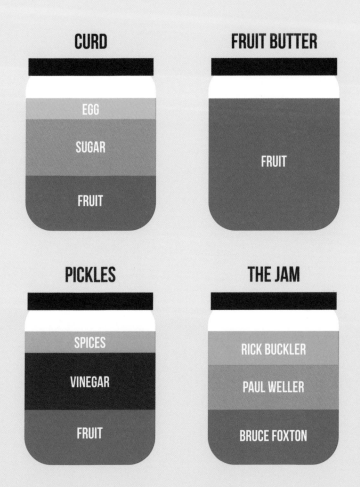

CURD

EGG

SUGAR

FRUIT

FRUIT BUTTER

FRUIT

PICKLES

SPICES

VINEGAR

FRUIT

THE JAM

RICK BUCKLER

PAUL WELLER

BRUCE FOXTON

CROQUES

French breakfast items, with or without the beret.

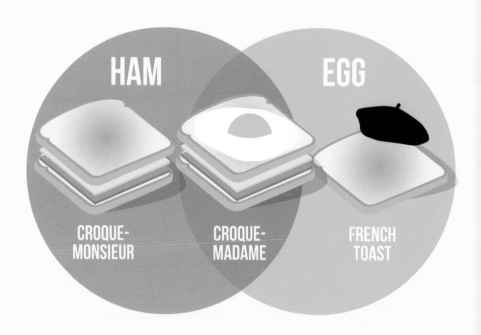

HAM

EGG

CROQUE-
MONSIEUR

CROQUE-
MADAME

FRENCH
TOAST

RUDE SEAFOOD

Disgusting.

MOBY
DICK

POOP
DECK

SPERM
WHALE

OCEAN

POLLOCK

TURTLE
HEAD

CRABS

COCKLES
& WINKLES

BROWN
TROUT

RIVER

CHUB
SUCKER

FRESH WATER
CLAM

SHELLFISH

RED
SNAPPER

BOTTOM
FEEDERS

HOW TO CUT TOAST

The toast rack is the ideal way to cool hot, delicious toast into inedible blocks of cardboard. Thank you B & B owners, thank you very much.

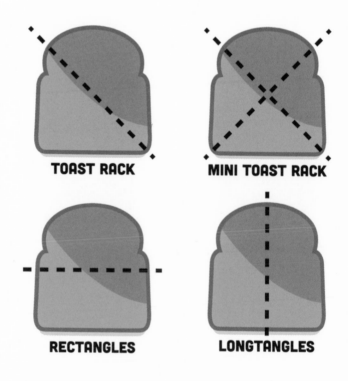

TOAST RACK

MINI TOAST RACK

RECTANGLES

LONGTANGLES

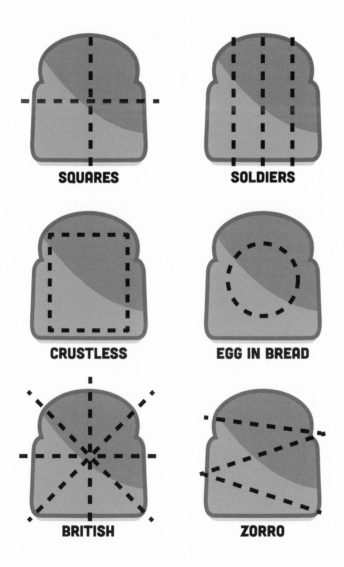

SQUARES

SOLDIERS

CRUSTLESS

EGG IN BREAD

BRITISH

ZORRO

SAUCY

As long as it's brown sauce on a bacon butty.

KETCHUP

BURGER

BROWN

MARIE
ROSE

MAYO

CAESAR

WORCESTER-
SHIRE

THE IMPORTANCE OF COLOUR

PARSNIP

SNOWMAN'S
NOSE

BRITISH REGIONAL FRIED BREAKFASTS

Bacon, eggs, mushrooms, tomatoes and fried bread are all standard.
Here are the regional variations...

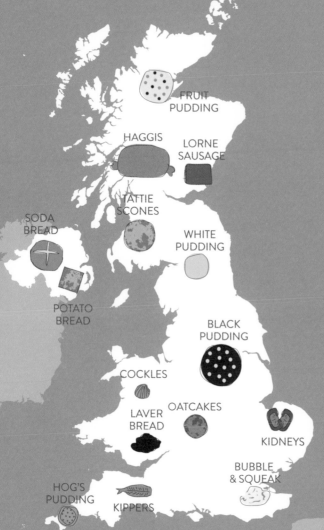

FRUIT
PUDDING

HAGGIS

LORNE
SAUSAGE

SODA
BREAD

TATTIE
SCONES

WHITE
PUDDING

POTATO
BREAD

BLACK
PUDDING

COCKLES

OATCAKES

LAVER
BREAD

KIDNEYS

BUBBLE
& SQUEAK

HOG'S
PUDDING

KIPPERS

SPOONS BY SOCIAL CLASS

stirs tea with runcible spoon

Silver → Caviar
Absinthe → Runcible
Soup → Egg
Teaspoon → Egg
Dessert → Coffee
Sundae → Ladle
Wooden → Tablespoon
Disposable → Uri Geller
Souvenir spoon → Spork
Greasy → Cocaine
Heroin → Cocaine

WAX CHEESE CHART

● Amount of cheese wrapped
● Amount of cheese unwrapped

THE BRITISH CHEESE SPECTRUM

BLUENESS

SOMERSET
BRIE

STINKING
BISHOP

LANCASHIRE

WENSLEYDALE

DOUBLE
GLOUCESTER

RED
LEICESTER

BLUE
VINNEY

CHEDDAR

STILTON

YARG

CAERPHILLY

HARDNESS

HOW DO YOU LIKE YOUR EGGS?

I like them Fabergé.

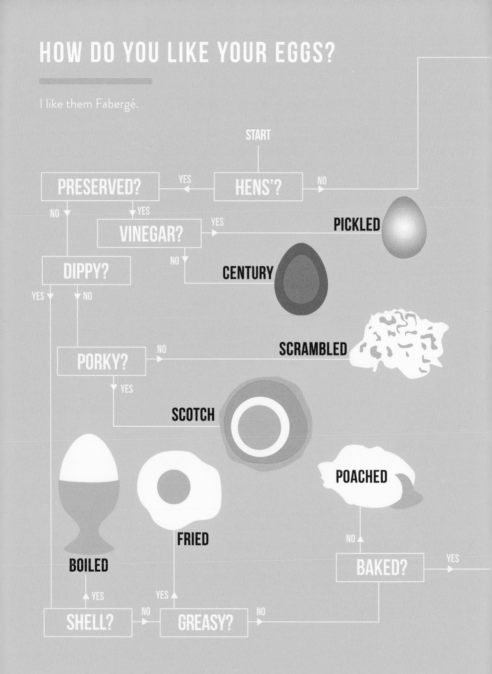

START

PRESERVED? — YES → HENS'? — NO →

PICKLED

VINEGAR? — YES →

CENTURY

PORKY? — NO →

SCRAMBLED

SCOTCH

POACHED

BOILED

FRIED

BAKED? — YES →

SHELL? — NO → GREASY? — NO →

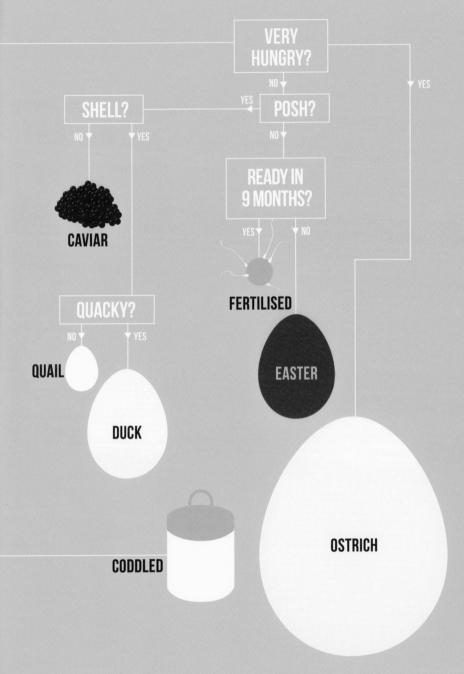

SHOULD I GET A TAKEAWAY?

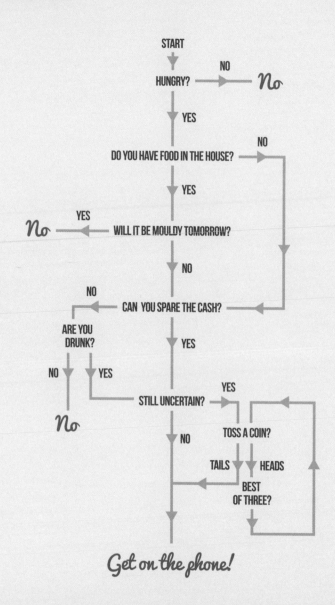

START

HUNGRY? → NO → *No*

YES

DO YOU HAVE FOOD IN THE HOUSE? → NO

YES

No ← YES ← WILL IT BE MOULDY TOMORROW?

NO

CAN YOU SPARE THE CASH? → NO

ARE YOU DRUNK?

NO   YES

No

YES

STILL UNCERTAIN? → YES

TOSS A COIN?

NO

TAILS   HEADS

BEST OF THREE?

Get on the phone!

OK, BUT WHICH TAKEAWAY?

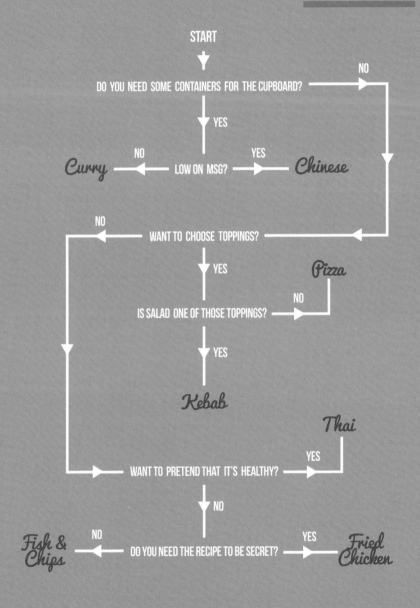

START

DO YOU NEED SOME CONTAINERS FOR THE CUPBOARD? → NO

YES

Curry ← NO — LOW ON MSG? — YES → Chinese

NO ← WANT TO CHOOSE TOPPINGS?

YES

Pizza

IS SALAD ONE OF THOSE TOPPINGS? — NO →

YES

Kebab

Thai

WANT TO PRETEND THAT IT'S HEALTHY? — YES →

NO

Fish & Chips ← NO — DO YOU NEED THE RECIPE TO BE SECRET? — YES → Fried Chicken

LAYERED PUDDINGS

Puddings with layers.

TRIFLE

KNICKERBOCKER
GLORY

TIRAMISU

STRAWBERRY
CHEESECAKE

LEMON
MERINGUE

BANOFFEE

CUSTARD SLICE

CRÈME BRÛLÉE

BLACK FOREST
GATEAU

MERINGUE /ICING	CREAM	ICE CREAM /CREAM CHEESE	CUSTARD	LEMON CURD	BANANA	SPONGE/ PASTRY
CARAMEL	BURNT SUGAR	CHOCOLATE	COFFEE	JELLY	STRAW- BERRY	CHERRY

LAYERED LUNCH

Lunches with layers.

LASAGNE

MOUSSAKA

BLT

CROQUE-MONSIEUR

HAMBURGER

CLUB

PIZZA

ELVIS

COTTAGE PIE

LETTUCE	BANANA	CHEESE	MUSTARD	WHITE SAUCE/ MAYO	MASH	PASTA/ BREAD
CHICKEN	PEANUT BUTTER	BEEF	LAMB	BACON/ HAM	AUBERGINE	TOMATO

THII

NGS

CIGAR LIFESPAN

All the bravado and hilarious Churchill impressions after lighting a cigar at a social function quickly ebb away as the reality of the situation creeps up on you. First the coughing, then the nausea. If you can last to the vomit stage then you are a better man than I.

BIG PIMPIN'

ACCEPTANCE

COUGHING

IMPRESSIONS
Hannibal, Churchill,
Groucho Marx...

Time

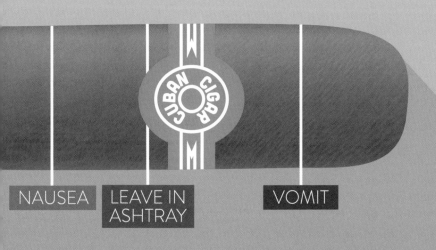

NAUSEA

LEAVE IN ASHTRAY

VOMIT

BEARS

Koalas are a law unto themselves.

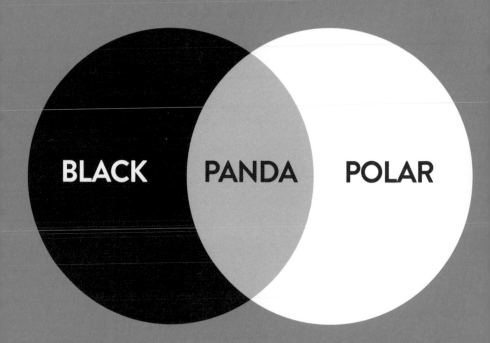

BLACK   PANDA   POLAR

HITLER

BRAZILIAN HITLER

HOLLYWOOD HITLER

COMMON NANNY NARRATIVES

Arrives, sings and leaves.

McPHEE   POPPINS   MARIA

ARRIVES

SINGS

DOES MAGIC

MARRIES

LEAVES

COMMON FAIRYTALE NARRATIVES

Houses in the woods are never good news.

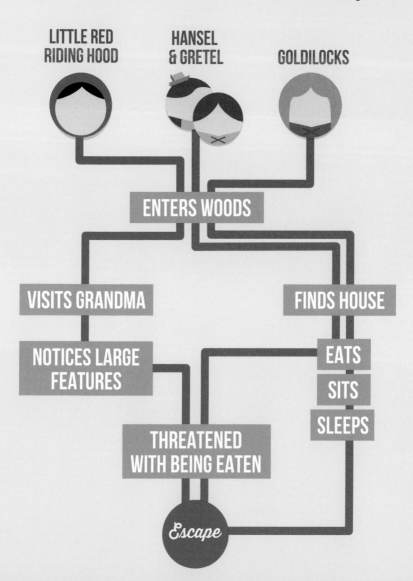

LITTLE RED RIDING HOOD

HANSEL & GRETEL

GOLDILOCKS

ENTERS WOODS

VISITS GRANDMA

FINDS HOUSE

NOTICES LARGE FEATURES

EATS

SITS

SLEEPS

THREATENED WITH BEING EATEN

Escape

COMMON FAIRYTALE NARRATIVES 2

Princess edition.

COMMON FAIRYTALE NARRATIVES 3

Ugly, kiss, handsome.

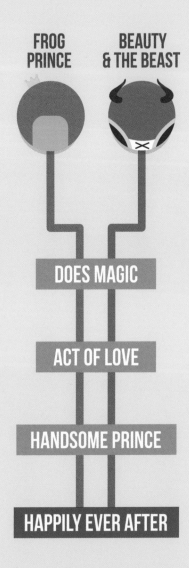

FROG
PRINCE

BEAUTY
& THE BEAST

DOES MAGIC

ACT OF LOVE

HANDSOME PRINCE

HAPPILY EVER AFTER

NELSON VS NAPOLEON

Two great leaders, but only one has a mighty column.

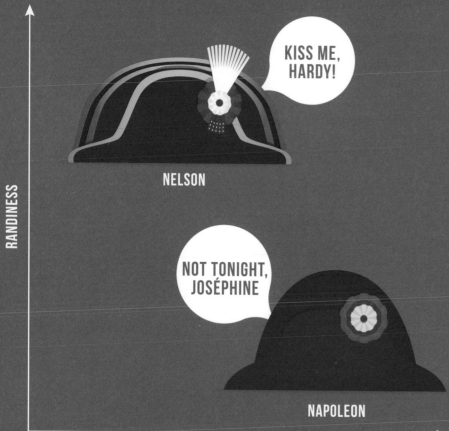

RANDINESS

AMOUNT OF ARMS

Disgusting.

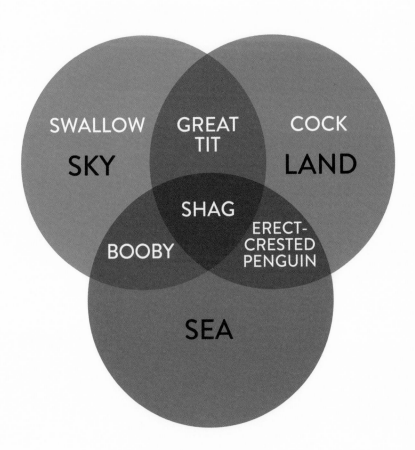

SWALLOW   GREAT   COCK
              TIT
SKY   LAND

            SHAG
                    ERECT-
  BOOBY   CRESTED
                   PENGUIN

         SEA

THE IMPORTANCE OF COLOUR

Always double check.

ICEBERG

SHARK

PINCHY AND STINGY

Scorpions are just the front end of a lobster and the
back end of a wasp stitched together by a madman.

PROSP-HAIR-ITY

Men's hair length is linked to the economy.
Boom times see long locks and bust is a return to a close trim.

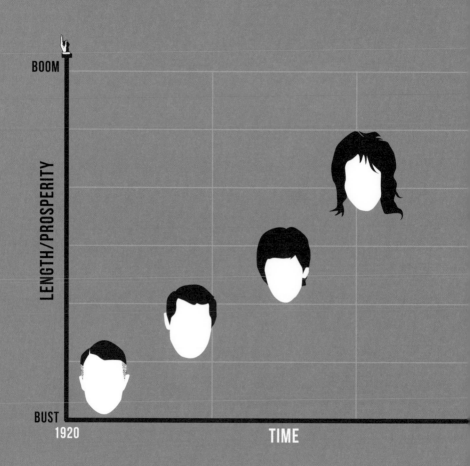

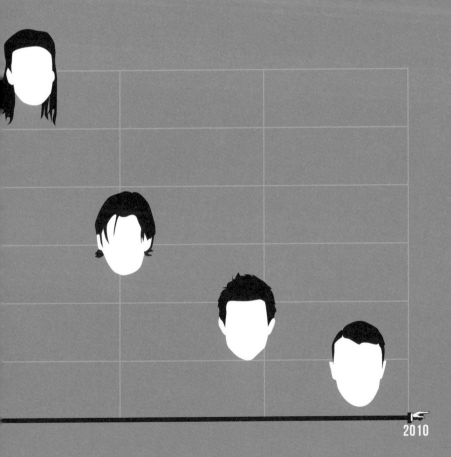

2010

HEMLINE INDEX

In times of decline, the hemline moves towards the floor (decreases),
and when the economy is booming, skirts get shorter and the hemline increases.

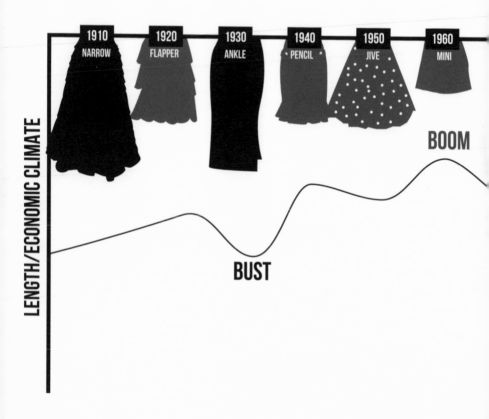

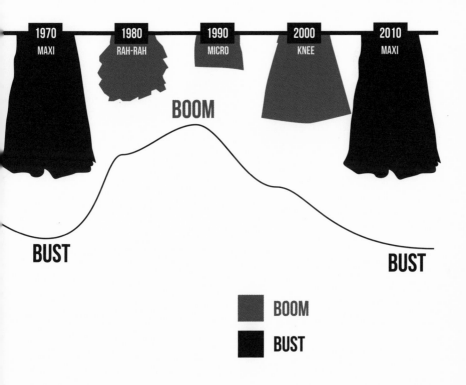

1970
MAXI

1980
RAH-RAH

1990
MICRO

2000
KNEE

2010
MAXI

BOOM

BUST

BUST

BOOM

BUST

BOWLING SHOES EXPLAINED

Part pope, part Elvis.

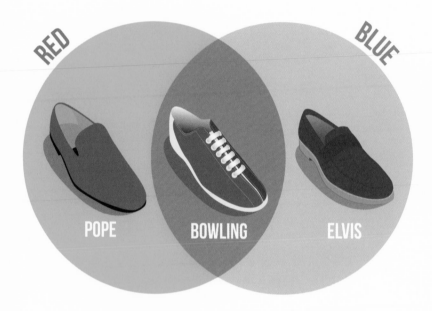

RED   BLUE

POPE   BOWLING   ELVIS

LOUBOUTIN SHOES EXPLAINED

Part Christian, part **FABULOUS!**

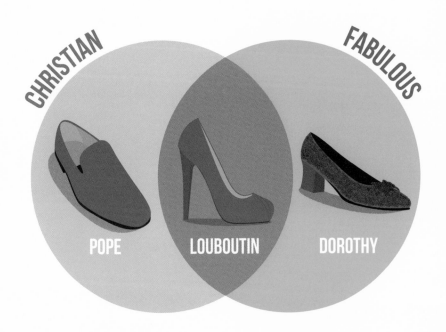

CHRISTIAN

FABULOUS

POPE

LOUBOUTIN

DOROTHY

BALLGAMES BY POSHNESS

Anyone for wiff waff?

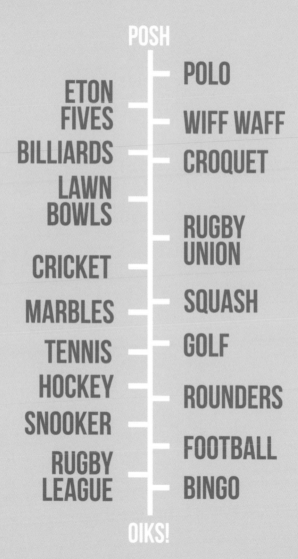

POSH

ETON
FIVES

BILLIARDS

LAWN
BOWLS

CRICKET

MARBLES

TENNIS

HOCKEY

SNOOKER

RUGBY
LEAGUE

POLO

WIFF WAFF

CROQUET

RUGBY
UNION

SQUASH

GOLF

ROUNDERS

FOOTBALL

BINGO

OIKS!

WHICH NECKWEAR TO WEAR?

It's always a toss-up between a cravat and a keyboard tie.

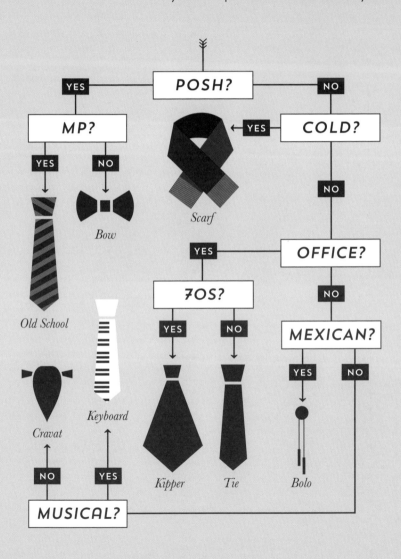

POSH?

YES — MP?

COLD?

NO

YES

MP?

YES — Old School

NO — Bow

YES — Scarf

Scarf

NO

OFFICE?

YES — 70S?

NO — MEXICAN?

70S?

YES — Kipper

NO — Tie

MEXICAN?

YES — Bolo

NO

Old School

Keyboard

Cravat

Kipper

Tie

Bolo

MUSICAL?

NO — Cravat

YES — Keyboard

SCIE

NCE

GAME THEORY

Family fun games in a 7-circle Venn diagram. BUCKAROO!

FINGER DEXTERITY

NOISY FINALE

BUCKAROO

HUNGRY HIPPOS

KER-PLUNK

OPER-ATION

JENGA

MARBLES/ COUNTERS

HASBRO

TIDDLY WINKS

GAME THEORY

BOP IT

OTHELLO

RUBIK'S CUBE

CONNECT FOUR

CLUEDO

GUESS WHO?

STRATEGY

MATCHING COLOURS/ FACES

BATTLE-SHIP

MASTER-MIND

MAKING CONNECTIONS

EULER DIETGRAM

Cannibals have the most varied diet.

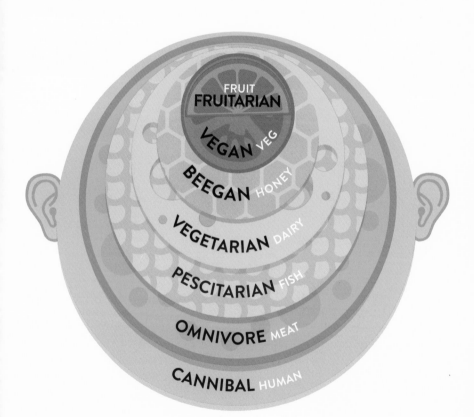

FRUIT
FRUITARIAN

VEGAN VEG

BEEGAN HONEY

VEGETARIAN DAIRY

PESCITARIAN FISH

OMNIVORE MEAT

CANNIBAL HUMAN

MANIMALS

What do you get if you cross a man with...

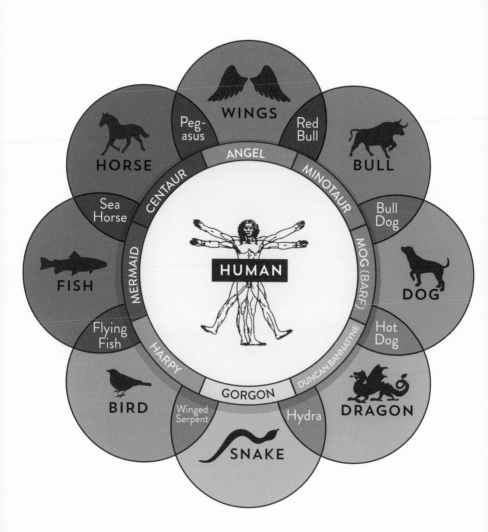

BASEBALL CAP ROTATION

Fashions change, and with them the
angle of the baseball cap over the decades.

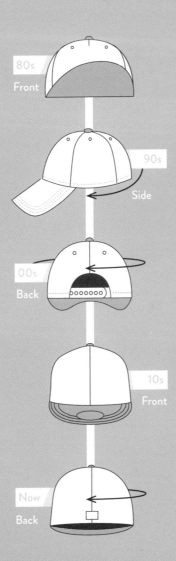

80s
Front

90s
Side

00s
Back

10s
Front

Now
Back

THE GRAND UNICYCLE THEORY

The theory that Einstein hypothesised and many have since sought is finally here. Enjoy.

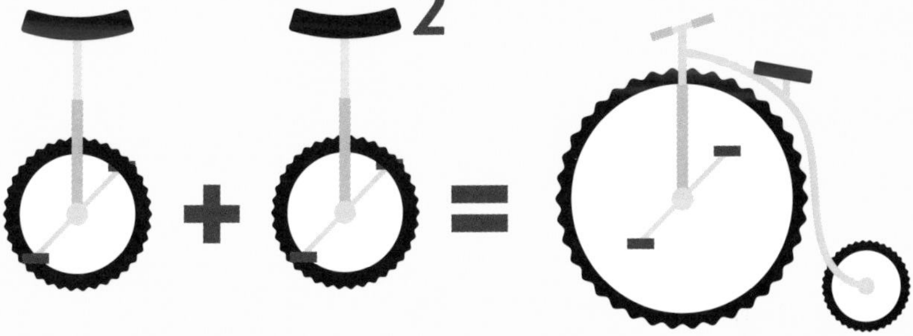

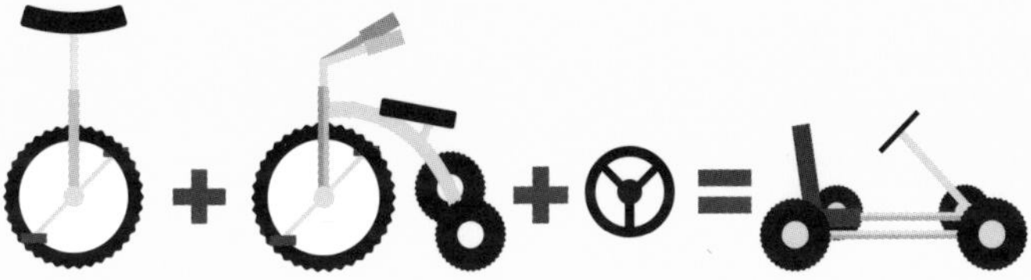

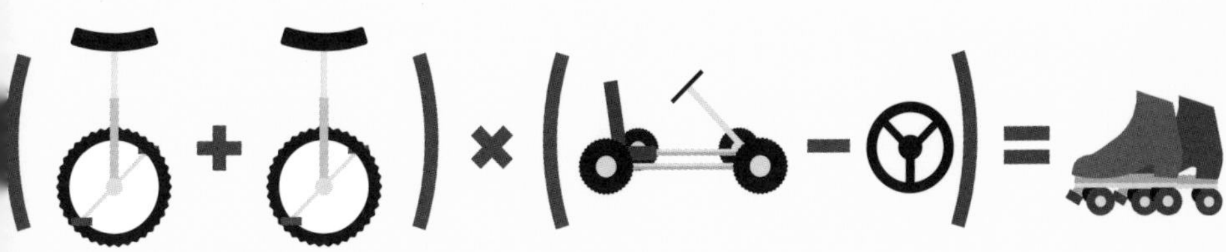

WITCH MORAL COMPASS

Good Witch
of the North

N

Ethically Challenged
Witch of the North West

NW

Moderate Witch
of the North East

NE

Wicked Witch
of the West

W

WITCH
MORAL
COMPASS

E

Wicked Witch
of the East

SW

Unpredictable Witch
of the South West

SE

Changeable Witch
of the South East

S

Good Witch
of the South

THE WORKING DAY

The length of the average working day.

STONE AGE

STUDENT

OFFICE AGE

INDUSTRIAL AGE

16 HOURS

3 HOURS

5 HOURS

8 HOURS

THE HOKEY-COKEY CHART

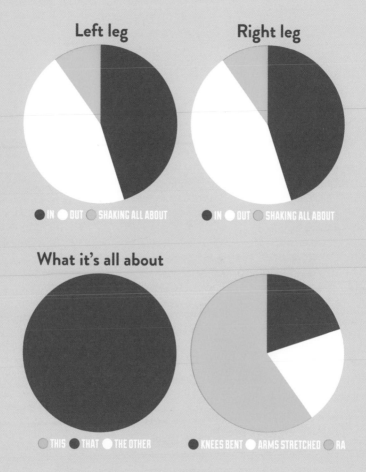

Left leg

● IN ● OUT ● SHAKING ALL ABOUT

Right leg

● IN ● OUT ● SHAKING ALL ABOUT

What it's all about

● THIS ● THAT ● THE OTHER

● KNEES BENT ● ARMS STRETCHED ● RA

Pirates

1

2
Birds

3 Cameras

Mammals
4

0
Students

SPIDER DIAGRAM
Number
of legs?

5
Starfish

+
Creepy

10
Fruits de mer

7 Broken
spider

Beetles

8
Spiders

6

GREEN POWERS

If only Superman knew that Popeye had the antidote!

SCIENCE VENN

The three main fields of science boiled down to their essences. Which biophysicist hasn't considered making a helicopter from the remains of a beloved pet?

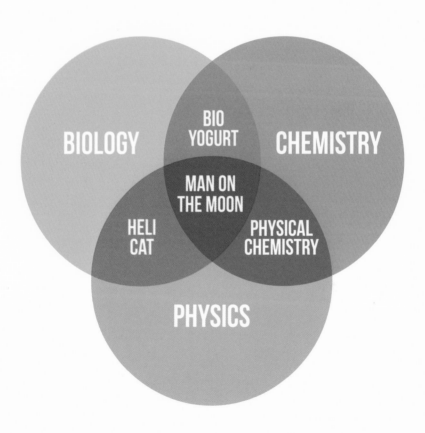

LOADING BARS

Both take around 5 minutes. Only one can kill you though.
Loading bars are dangerous.

LOADING

SMOKING

BUFFER RINGS

Web developers! Liven up a buffering
experience with some simple colour amends.

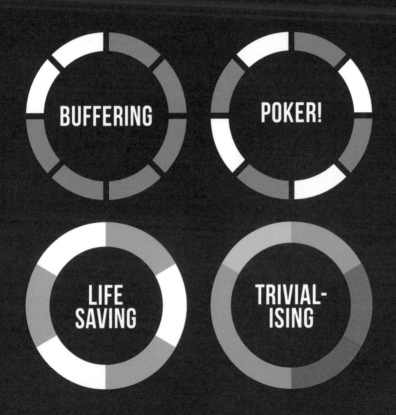

BUFFERING

POKER!

LIFE
SAVING

TRIVIAL-
ISING

DECISIONS, DECISIONS

I'm guessing it's already too late?

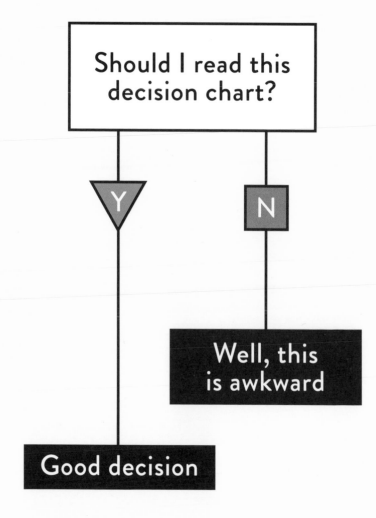

Should I read this decision chart?

Y

N

Good decision

Well, this is awkward

GARDEN UTENSIL EQUATION

Should be called a spake really.

REGIONAL EXCLAMATIONS

OCH AYE!

WEY AYE!

EY UP!

OH!

OOH ARR!

ARR!

OOH
LA LA!

STOOL CHART

Ever tried to pass a tricky Type 2?

FIRMNESS

HEIGHT

TYPE 2

TYPE 3

TYPE 6

TYPE 4

TYPE 7

TYPE 5

TYPE 1

HOLI

DAYS

SNOW VENN

Also how King Wenceslas likes his pizza...

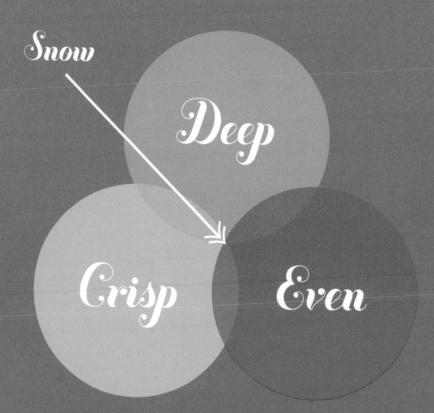

Snow

Deep

Crisp

Even

THE SANTA VENN DIAGRAM

Nobody expects the Spanish Inquisition.

GREAT POWER, GREAT RESPONSIBILTY

GOD

SUPER HERO

SANTA

KNOWS IF YOU HAVE BEEN NAUGHTY OR NICE

SPANISH INQUISITION

WEARS RED SUIT

CHRISTMAS NIGHTS

Are often...

'TIS THE SEASON TO BE JOLLY

I bet you counted them.

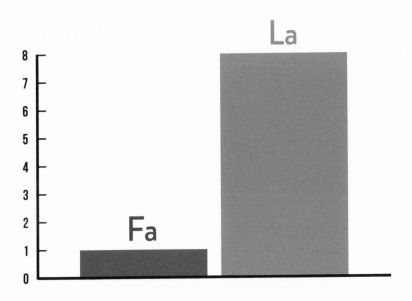

FIND YOUR FESTIVE FOWL

Which bird to choose for Christmas dinner?

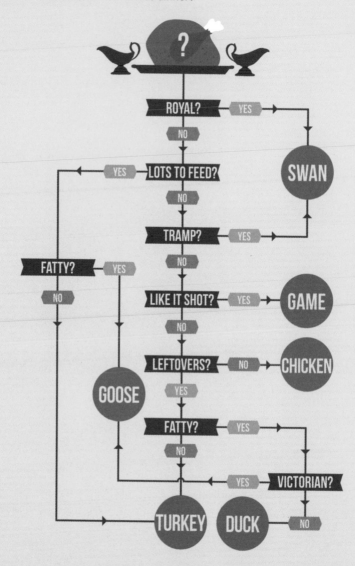

ROYAL? — YES → SWAN

NO

LOTS TO FEED? — YES →

NO

TRAMP? — YES →

NO

FATTY? — YES →

NO

LIKE IT SHOT? — YES → GAME

NO

LEFTOVERS? — NO → CHICKEN

YES

GOOSE

FATTY? — YES →

NO

VICTORIAN? — YES →

NO

TURKEY   DUCK

FIND YOUR FESTIVE FOWL (VEGETARIAN)

With apologies to vegetarians.

?

ROYAL?

NO

LOTS TO FEED?

NO

TRAMP?

NO

LIKE IT SHOT?

NO

LEFTOVERS?

YES

FATTY?

NO

NUT ROAST

THE IMPORTANCE OF FESTIVE COLOUR

Be careful what you hang on the tree.

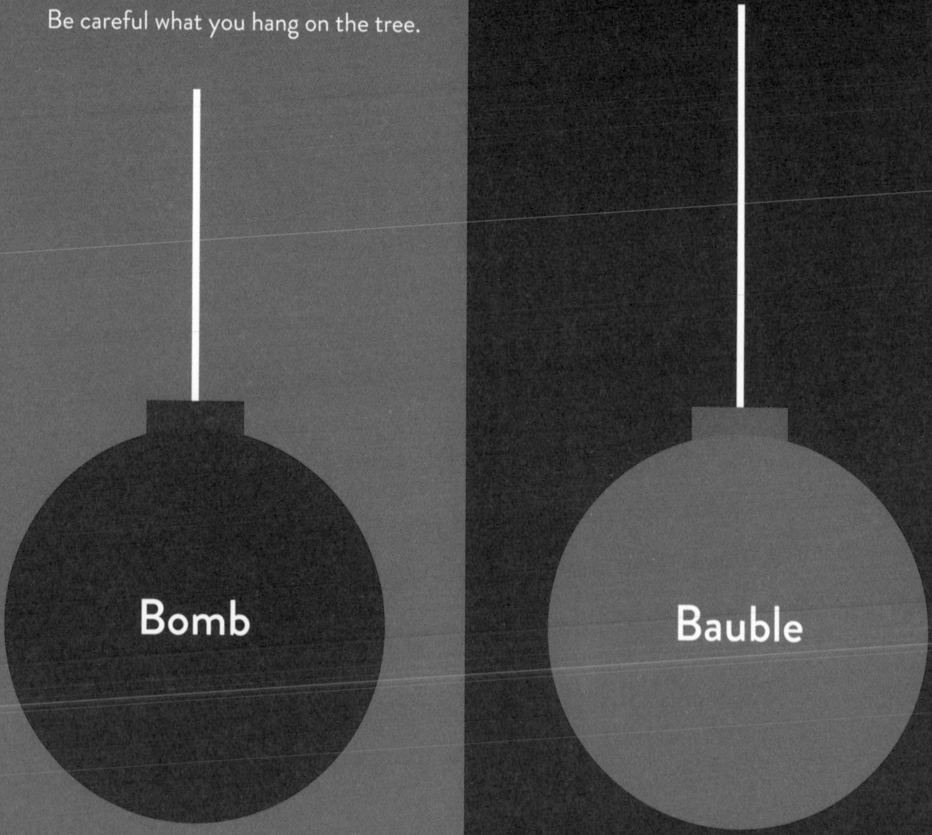

Bomb

Bauble

THE EASTER VENNY

The luckier among you will have trodden in a 'dog egg'
or found a present from your cat on the doormat.

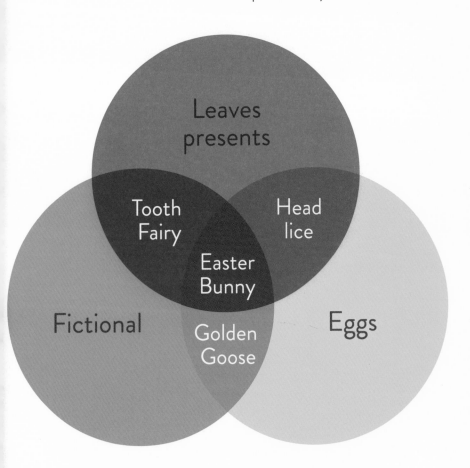

Leaves presents

Tooth Fairy

Head lice

Easter Bunny

Fictional

Golden Goose

Eggs

If you're interested in finding out more about our books,
find us on Facebook at **Summersdale Publishers**
and follow us on Twitter at **@Summersdale**.

www.summersdale.com